# saints and seagulls

### poems and images
## Ann Marie Boyden

### edited by Annetta Link

∞ INFINITY
PUBLISHING

ISBN 978-0-7414-9728-4  Paperback
ISBN 978-0-7414-9729-1  eBook
Library of Congress Control Number: 2013912027

Printed in the United States of America

Published November 2013

INFINITY PUBLISHING
1094 New DeHaven Street, Suite 100
West Conshohocken, PA 19428-2713
Toll-free (877) BUY BOOK
Local Phone (610) 941-9999
Fax (610) 941-9959
Info@buybooksontheweb.com
www.buybooksontheweb.com

**With thanks to:**

Kathleen, supportive and enthusiastic –
AnnEtta, the very best of very best friends –
Professor Diana Martin, who got me to write poems again –
Susan Wanlass, PhD, for the last word.

# TABLE OF CONTENTS

# PREFACE

Because my best friend asked me to, I'm writing a preface to the first published collection of her poems. Ann Marie has always had a strong creative side which found expression through performing as a student or member of a community company, establishing and running a successful advertising agency, and then as Executive Director of the American Institute of Architects Trust. Retirement gave her the opportunity to focus on two art forms, her poems and her photographs, that had long been sources of personal satisfaction to her and a special treat to the friends with whom she shared them. Now she's ready to share her work with more of us. Several of her poems and photographs included here have won prizes and awards. Each of them has something significant to say.

**AnnEtta and Ann(a) Marie back at the Pi Phi House.**

You don't need to know much more about Ann Marie to enjoy her poetry, but I think you should know that she was raised and spent the first part of her professional life in Salt Lake City, Utah. That's where I met her in high school, where we went to college together, and where we developed a friendship that has lasted a lifetime. Growing up in a predominantly Mormon community with their tradition of respect for hard work and self-reliance was a significant influence on Ann Marie. So also was the beauty of the Salt Lake valley, particularly the Wasatch and Oquirrh Mountain Ranges that ring much of the valley and make you feel both humble and protected.

I am extraordinarily proud of Ann Marie and her work. This collection has allowed me to remember how special it has been to share the goofiness, the woes, and the triumphs of living – even a continent apart – with my best friend. We are both enthusiastic about this collection and invite you now to enjoy.


AnnEtta Link
San Rafael, California
April 2013

## Saints and Seagulls

AMBoyden

Just look at you,
cocky and confident
as when you saved
the crops from the crickets.

Cheeky gulls suspended above
sea and sand anticipating
a scrap of semolina.
Son of the sky.

Daughter of the sea.
At the Chesapeake's mouth,
down at the dump,
in the straits of Mackinac,

out in the parking lot,
over the Golden Gate,
ubiquitous ancient acrobats
sent to save the Saints.

Insatiable flying jesters
with big knees and clown feet,
you know the insects are God's too.
Clamoring gulls crying

out for more, darting
dodging, screaming shanties
from an inland sea where you
are supposed to have

rescued Mormons from starvation.
The Saints remember you.
They remember the wings.
Their children remember

and their children's children.
Do you know why the good
gulls, the State Birds of Utah,
are called California Seagulls,

but those bad bugs,
some kind of giant killer katydids,
are called Mormon Crickets?

*Unlike some of the others, Great
Smoky Mountains National Park
on the border between Tennessee and
North Carolina has no entry fee. The
hostess at the Visitors' Center explains why:*

AMBoyden

## In Her Own Words

"Tain't how it growed up. Federal din't
put much in. Both states put up money
and moved folks right outta there.
'Tain't right to charge 'em to come

back in, what with all their kin to bury
n'all. Up there still air home places
'n', churches, graveyards' 'n' barns.
You can go up in there to the Cove

'n' mostly see what it was back then.
When clouds come down and the wind
blows you can hear their voices.
I swear you can hear 'em cryin' out."

*Cade's Cove, Tennessee*

3

# From Hollows

Hear them singing
five hundred families
from hollows and coves.

Watch the women,
simple dresses covered
with gingham aprons

fixing meager meals
out of nothing but pride.
Hear them singing.

Watch the little girl with
a corncob doll and the
boy with a stick.

See wide suspenders
on men too thin for their
overalls. Hunt with them.

Follow them to unyielding
fields of scrawny corn.
Hear them singing.

Smell the wood smoke
gray as their ghosts
from chimneys and stills.

Taste the raw whiskey
crude and white
burning empty bellies.

They came west from
Jamestowne. Came west
to settle near springs

and streams far from
the outside currents
for two hundred years

only to be displaced.
Now seventy summers gone
you can hear them singing.

## Is Halley's Comet Coming Back?

Mother made pot roast the night Halley's Comet
was to appear in the sky above our little town.
There were fresh vegetables, mashed potatoes and gravy.
"Sit down. We're saying the blessing,"
Father said, "The comet will wait."
It didn't.

Our brother graduated on the day John Gielgud
was reading Shakespeare at the Capitol theatre.
Instead of hearing Gielgud we saw our brother walk
across a stage and be called "Doctor,"
for the first time. John Gielgud will wait.
He didn't.

Father was in the hospital the Sunday the Redskins
won the Super Bowl. We gave the tickets away,
scalped them actually, to fly out and be with him.
It was absolutely the right thing and we thought
we were glad we did it. The Redskins will wait.
They didn't.

The day the Queen came to town, we didn't see her.
Our sister's garden was in the neighborhood show.
We mowed and groomed and edged. The lawn tractor
broke down. I found a man to fix it. We finished
just in time. The Queen will wait.
She didn't.

The dinner is over. The Doctor is out forever.
Father will not be coming back,
so far neither have the Redskins.
But there is peace in our sister's garden,
without grief or guilt or remorse. It remains,
with blooming perennials, mature plantings
and the sound of water,
fit for a Queen.

# Dodging and Burning

The first time I saw someone dodge
and burn a silver gelatin print, it was enchanting.
Beneath the enlarger, as seconds ticked,
it was as if he held tangible light in his hands
shading the picture to reinforce
the lie that all photographs are.

Later I held the light myself. After years
of testing images, changing exposures,
burning and dodging, bathing in chemicals
until the print is perfect…or not. No matter.
Just toss it and begin a new one
from the same negative.

It's too bad everything can't be like printing
from film negatives onto silver gelatin.
Dodge the dark places, bring out the detail.
Burn the sallow, make it strong.
Dodge too little, burn too much,
start over.

*Coalville, Utah Circa 1900 from original*          **WMBoyden negative**

## House Cleaning

Because the board of health
would have come to
close me down
today I cleaned my house.
And because of the
aloneness, too,
for had someone, anyone,
called I would have gone,
leaving the dust and grime,
the rain spotted windows,
the crumbs of dog biscuits
on the floor. The plants
unwatered.

But no one called, and so
today I cleaned my house.

## House Cleaning 2

The woman who was once my friend asks,
"Are you dating?" I am surprised
We have not seen each other for years.
I mumble, "Not really."
"I hear there aren't many single men there,
and the ones who are there, are gay," she says.

I don't respond.
I'm back in high school dating an
ROTC Officer when it is not
fashionable at all.
She has been married for forever.
She tells everyone that
her husband brings her lattes and
newspapers in bed.

As romantic as that sounds,
I don't know if I'd like it.
Seems way too Jackie Collins,
and after all it may not be true.
I've dated and am done with it.
Finished.

If something happens, well, who knows?
In the meantime the best times are:
me and my dog.
me and my camera.
me with my pad and pen.
I am very good company.
Ask my dog.

If someone anyone called
I would say, "I'm sorry.
Today I'm cleaning my house.
The bridge group is coming on Friday."

# Idol Day Dreaming

**1955**
A girl watches the blond
singer on the small screen,
glorious in black and white.
*"You sigh the song begins,
you speak and I hear violins..."*
She wants not to be here
in this tired and tepid place.
She hears the sultry voice
and lush orchestration
on tiny tinny speakers.
*Romance on the High Seas.*
She wants to be blond,
wants to hear violins,
wants to feel *"It's Magic,"*
wants to be the singer.

**2010**
A boy watches the man
with spiked hair gyrate
in digital color on a big screen.
*"Given' yourself to me, baby,
Can never be wrong."*
He wants not to be here
in this trite and tedious place.
He hears the rasping voice
and battering beat
in Bose surround sound.
*"Come on, come on, come on..."*
and wants to *Get It On.*
Wants instant celebrity,
wants to chant *"S'all right now,"*
wants to be the Idol.

## Seven Photographs

Hanging on the wall
in a gallery
seven photographs,
seven of my photographs.
Seven selected from
hundreds of images.
Nervous and excited
I delivered them,
matted and framed.
Laid them tenderly on the floor.
Are they the best of the hundreds?
I don't think so.
Are they even good?
I don't know.
They must be good because now
they are hanging on the wall
in the Studio School Gallery
at the Virginia Museum of Fine Arts.
That's good. Isn't it?

**AMBoyden**

# Alone In the City

Feeling martini sophisticated,
anonymous, and free
in the city,
alone at Sardi's
surrounded by
Hirschfeld faces
and the giant backdrop
of the Shubert marquee
across 44$^{th}$ Street.
People at the next
table from New Jersey,
in town for a show,
want to talk. You don't.

Walk cross town
back to the hotel
on crowded sidewalks
full of spirits and shadows
in the after-theater night.
Never think it might
not be safe.

In the cavernous
lobby the sounds
from the piano bar
echo. The elevator
climbs to room service.
No one to call.

## Twelfth-Grade English

Pansy Powell's first period English:
all the cool kids were there. Football
and basketball jocks, track stars,

cheerleaders, prom and drama queens.
Surprisingly, most of them studied.
There were a few of the rest: squares,

lunchers, cornballs. Members of the
Marching Band, and ROTCies, both in
uniform. A greaser was in uniform too:

Elvis hair, tight Levi's, and leather jacket.
Some of the rest did not study at all.
By tall windows in western winter light,

sat two who thought they were writers,
listening carefully as Miss Powell stood
at the blackboard where a weird poem

was written in white chalk and Middle
English. "*The Canterbury Tales* is one
of the greatest poems ever written,"

she said. The assignment: memorize
these eighteen lines of the prologue –
be prepared to recite it – with correct

pronunciation. Miss Powell demonstrated.
More than half actually memorized it,
the first person called on to recite had not.

The next two, both ROTCies, had.
A clarinet player, a square, the greaser,
and the writers all struggled through it.

A jock recited fast enough to set a record.
A drama queen ACTED! I was in that class
and still remember - the first four lines anyway.

## Class Reunion

One woman says,
"You look better than
you ever have!"
as if it were a compliment.
She certainly doesn't
look better or worse,
only old.

There are so very
many old people here,
some looking old,
most just being old.
These people don't cheer.
and they don't sing,

unless they are alumni
of the a capella choir.
Then they sing. Looking
down on the rest of us
just as they did all
those years ago.

**Lignell and Gill**

## MOTHER USED TO WRITE POETRY

When she was young, college young,
Mother used to write poetry.
Her poems were good for sure because
the only known examples were
published in *Utah Sings:*
*An Anthology of Contemporary Verse.*
It was Nineteen Thirty Something.

The poems are a little stiff and quite formal.
But hey, they didn't always rhyme,
the voice was clear, the diction strong.
She stopped writing poetry when she married.
She always said that Father made her quit.
Sort of like smoking, I guess, but
no one in our family smoked.

Father always said it was only fair since
Mother made him give up hunting,
although he may have just lost interest.
Today is her birthday and I wonder if her literary
identity, voice, and passion were stacked up
in the basement like Father's guns --
only invisible

## Dead Butterflies

You showed me butterflies
dried, dead, done up
in plastic envelopes

but the vibrant colors
in the stained glass
were deep and rich.

The designs intricate,
defined as when
the cocoon hatched

the winged thing into
a world not really fit
for such delicate beauty

yet there it is,
in the envelope
the spirit long gone,

the will and soul of
fluttering flight gone.
The beauty, the art

remaining to remind
us that love need
not be that way.

Need it?

The spirit can stay
along with the beauty.

Can't it?

## At the Museum of Modern Art
## No Flash Please

People taking pictures
of pictures
of paintings
of sculpture.
Take pictures of
people taking pictures
of pictures
of paintings
of sculpture
MeO, MyO MoMA!
Who's seeing *The Starry Night?*

All images: AMBoyden

***The Starry Night***, <u>Vincent van Gogh</u>, 1889,
<u>Museum of Modern Art</u> , New York City

Were the violent voices
you heard coming
from shooting stars
and another world
somewhere in the cosmos?
What sounds do china blue
like your eyes,
sunflower yellow like
the bees and the pollen,
sea foam green from your
distant past
make above the town
and your asylum?
Is it the noise in your ear –
a hiss, a whistle, a throb?
Or is it the voice of God
in your head
before you cut off your ear?
Are the colors silent now?

*Dieppe, Bassin Duquesne, low tide, morning sun.*
Camille Pissarro, 1937, Musée d'Orsay, Paris

## The First Impressionist

Pissarro in the Caribbean
seeing beauty in the ordinary.
Pissarro at Eragny
seeing grace in labor.
Pissarro in London
seeing colors in the drab.
Tropical memories,
the exquisite light
reflected from paradise.
No wonder the others
began to see it too.
Cezanne saw it *en plein air.*
Monet, Degas, Renoir, Gauguin
guided through the landscape,
seeing the poems around them,
painting them.

*The Red Roofs,* Camille Pissarro, 1877, Musée d'Orsay, Paris

*The courtyard of the Pissarro Residence,*
*14 Donnigens Gade, Charlotte Amalie, USVI*

AMBoyden

## Piazza della Signoria

Drawn into the painting, you stand
in front of Palazzo Vecchio on
the Piazza della Signoria.

Sweaty tourists in rude tee shirts
fade and become knights and players.
The photo shop becomes an apothecary.

David, the symbol of Florentine freedom,
is where he belongs, outdoors,
in front of the Palazzo.

Stand in the Piazza della Signoria
across from the church of San Romolo
destroyed in the 18$^{th}$ century.

You are not here for cruel execution,
but for celebration, "Festival of the Tributes"
when cities pay tribute to the Prince.

The haunting nightmare of Savonarola is
gone, replaced with colorful banners,
musicians, dancers, and jubilant citizens.

Stand in the Piazza della Signoria to watch
floats and a parade of knights under the
soaring towers of the Badia and the Bargello.

Look out over the tiled roofs of Florence
to the fertile hills of Tuscany surrounding the city.
Then it is over, you are back in the gallery.

## Consternation

Cupids are often mistaken for angels
and placed on the ceilings of
Roman Catholic Churches,
causing consternation among the Clergy
who are ordained only to spiritual love.
They have taken vows, you know.
but so have the ancient gods
to make certain the mortals mate
producing both men and gods,
and one assumes women as well.
So it must be difficult for the Clergy,
especially if the sacramental wine
Is a fine vintage,
to have the Roman God of erotic love
and his first cousin Eros,
whether or not they are armed with arrows,
hanging out under the rafters.

*Manga is the Japanese
word for comics.
At least that's what we're told.*

**Manga**
Japanese calligraphy
from 1798.

They are real.
with perfect faces,
and huge, dark, blank eyes.
Androgynous ones
with mops of spiked hair

and ragged bangs.
With flowing scarves
and puffed up jackets,
they are cross-dressers and flirts.
They are real,

consorting with rogue death gods.
Some possessed by animals
of the Chinese zodiac.
With long, long legs
they time travel

to meet ghosts and devils.
Some with gigantic thighs
dwell in the past and
are just visiting here.
They are real.

Half-demons and soul reapers,
finders of death notes.
They can be seen on the streets,
in the shops, in the schools.
They can be seen.

## Comics

"...in Afghanistan today"...
Morning comes, NPR intones
"Thousands are starving in the Sudan."
Find your slippers.
Is this milk sour?
How old are these Cheerios?
Turn on the TODAY Show,
"Eleven killed in bus crash"
"Kidnapped boy found dead."

Pick up the paper:
"16 Killed in Iraq"
"Body found in woods."
"Veterinarian loses dog."

Find Section D, quick!
Heart rate slows,
bood pressure lowers:
Satchel and Bucky are at it.
Rose is making hot cocoa.
Mike Patterson quit his job.
Dilbert confronts Dogbert.
*"The Dinette Set"* has
out uncouthed itself.
A dog in a lab coat
Is experimenting
In his basement to find,
squirrels afraid of heights!
Garfield spoiled Jon's date.
Oh No!
Laugh out loud.
OK. Face the day.

# A Miner's Request

*Diesel engine pulling one hundred cars,*
*one hundred hopper cars filled with coal.*

> *Think of me.*

Your radio comes on with news and music
and coffee is perked to welcome the day.
Open the fridge and push down the toaster.
Blow-dry your hair and dress for success.

> *Think of me.*

Computer lights up, records get made,
writing gets done, lunchtime is here.
Microwave whirrs, luncheon is served,
then back to the grind, working the phones.

> *Think of me.*

*Down in the dark is my life and my living,*
*down in the damp I deliver your day.*

> *Think of me.*

Stop for a drink. Laugh with your friends
playing bar trivia while watching a game.
Home again, whomp up some stir fry, fresh
from the freezer, eat it with chopsticks.

> *Think of me.*

Run the dishwasher, then the compactor.
Unload the dryer, load some CDs,
listen while reading a book on your nook.
Check the thermostat, turn off the lights.

> *Think of me.*

*Think of my family, the dead and the living,*
*think of my family today.*

## Summer Birthday

In the beginning there was ice cream.
Melting ice cream, smooth chocolate
in a matching sugar cone. And there
were amazing pink and green flowers
sprouting from a butter icing bed
on a devil's food foundation. A candle,
only one. For mid-July birthdays melt
the beginning into the ending, no matter
how tightly and carefully sticky fingers
hold onto the spoon.

# Popsicles

**AMBoyden**

They were almost always orange. Delightfully
artificial on a one hundred degree summer day
when Ned's experiment was to fry an egg on
the sidewalk in front of our house.

They cost a whole nickel but each half
had its own stick. So there was one for
me and one for Ned. He said that was
two-and-one-half cents apiece.

Usually they were found in the sub-zero
temperatures of the brand new freezer
chest at Princeton Market. I had to stand on
a crate to reach down in and grab one.

Sometimes they didn't have any at all.
Sometimes, not often, there would be
red ones that were supposed to be cherry.
Once there was one yellow banana tasting one!

But now they come in a box of twelve or
twenty-four with real fruit juice and vitamin C
but not as twins, just a phallic fruit dog on a stick.
They are also available in sugar free.

When consulted, Ned, now an important mathematician
with two PhDs, calculated that the average price is
sixteen-and-a-third cents. Thirty-two-and-two-thirds-cents
if they were still twins. But they're not.

Popsicles cost a whole six-times-plus as much
money and are probably better for children to eat,
but it's a shame they aren't the same.

27

## Wet Blanket

In a box somewhere there is a photograph of you,
or perhaps the picture is only in my mind.
You are sitting on the ugly, pink Danish modern
sofa my sorority sister gave me for that perfectly
awful apartment on F Street. You are sitting
there with a beer in your hand and a slice of
cold pizza on your bare knee. We've been
playing in the pool and your damp hair is pasted
to your head like a little boy's. Your wet trunks
are creating a surprise for the next person
to sit there.

I know now that this is the last time we'll be
together like this, with friends and beer and pizza
because although it was hard then —
it was right to tell you to get lost.
We were wasting our time – because
you thought I was wasting my time,
writing poetry.

*Water Lilies in the Rain*                                    AMBoyden

## Clearance

Once I was important, well paid, with great benefits
a well-appointed office, and a view of the monument.
When things became stressful, or political, or weird,
I said, "I'll go work in a bookstore." Now retired,
I do work in a bookstore. The assignment

today is setting up the clearance tables with more than
a thousand books. There are novels, cookbooks,
how-tos, and biographies of not-so-famous people.
Maybe they should be famous. Books about sports
and athletes are stacked with outdated computer

manuals, and travel guides for places people
don't go anymore. A memoir *Searching for the Sound:*
*My life with the Grateful Dead* is next to a volume
of someone's poetry. There's a thick one called
*An American Road Story* about two women on motorcycles.

A book titled *I was Howard Hughes* is appropriately
grouped with several of those smarmy volumes with titles
like *Your Inner "Whatever"* and *The Power of Nice.*
There are wine guides going back at least five years,
but not for last year. And here's the *New York City Library*

*Literary Companion.* A thousand books, each one written
by someone who celebrated when it was published,
being set out by a part time "book seller" in a college
bookstore. The only fanfare is a sign:

"CLEARANCE
# 75%
OFF LIST PRICE"

## How Much Longer?

At twenty-five there came a time
when you knew that you had lived
longer than you had yet to live.
You were either wrong or reckless.

At forty-five there came a time
when life seemed too good
to continue being so perfect.
You were either wrong or gullible.

At seventy there comes the time
when you know one is true,
or maybe the other - or perhaps
neither is the truth at all.

## Overheard at Dollywood

The man on the tram said to his friend:

*"She was a good country woman who named her sons
Francis, Shirley, Marion, and Clare."*

Why did she do it? Did she think it was elegant?
Was their father's name *Carroll*? Was it mischief
or just plain mean?

Or simply that she wanted daughters?

What do you suppose she would have named daughters:
Bobbie, Jackie, Frankie, and Jo?
Maybe Larry, Curley, and Mo.

## Bel Canto

In the recital hall a singer's hands flutter
articulating the essence of bel canto.
She is opening her soprano soul,
in a song of love and betrayal,
anger, death, and madness,
revealed by fluttering flutes
and mimicked cadenza.
Coloratura hands now waist high,
clutched, fingers wrapped 'round;
then flung out to the side.

Donizetti knew the truth:
high F natural is madness.

# TROUT TRIO

Once I loved a man
who played the string bass.
Second chair in the symphony.
I would watch as his big hand
moved the bow up and down
in unison with the first chair's.
And watch as his left hand
caressed the neck
pressing the strings
with tender passion.
I cherished that calloused hand,
how it felt on my skin.
I wondered at the precision
of his playing,
allowing the music to sweep
over our world and my life.
He was tall as double bass
players must be, and a little
stooped from leaning over the
big violin.
He would join his friends to play
The *Trout Quintet,*
"I get to be the trout"
he laughed, the joke reflected
in his dark brown eyes.
It was funny because
"trout" was what we called jerks,
and because Mother thought
he was a catch.
He owned an ancient yellow VW bug.
The three of us: he and the bass and I
would pile in and drive off, with the bass
Sticking out of the sun roof.
We went on adventures
involving an all-you-can-eat restaurant
And a performance.
A musician and a writer.
Then came the letter, "Greetings…"
and he had to go.
He died half way around the world ago.
Once I loved a man
who played the string bass.
We both lost him, the bass and I
in a stupid war
twice and a half way around the world ago.

## The Artist

The exterminator asks
"Web spiders or
Hunting spiders?"
An elaborate web
On the front porch
shimmers in the sun.
The spider moves toward
A mosquito at ten o'clock.
"Hunting spiders,
in the perennial garden.
Brown recluse could be
hiding in that shed,"
I say, knowing that
the spider on the porch
is an artist, a kindred.
An ally keeping bird flu
and malaria at bay.
It must be protected.

AMBoyden

## August Cornfield

When we were young
we took beer into
an August cornfield.
Lying in fertile furrows,
sinking into Weber Valley
we picked warm cobs
from the bottom of
towering stalks.
The smell of the silk
filling us with lust.
Shucking it,
feeding each other,
eating it raw,
washing it down
with warm beer
in the pristine
soil of Utah.
When we were young.

## Coven

Pentacle drawn on the floor.
bell, book, and candle.
Sleek black cat, Pyewacket,
broom, fire, and water.
Shadowy figures in black robes
spells, chants, and charms.
Hidden faces, sign of the goat
blood, brains, and bone.

## Thanksgiving with Friends

In November each year Gogie began
making her world-famous potato
cookies. It took hours.

Those cookies were part of
Thanksgiving and Christmas
for all of us - until last year.

Cousin Rosalind made them.
Now she's gone too. I miss her,
the cookies, not so much.

Having neither recipe nor time
for the cookies, I make Mother's shrimp
aspic and Aunt Helen's twice-baked

potatoes and look forward
to silver and crystal and china,
lace table cloths and linen napkins.

Making them with anticipation of
Thanksgiving with friends and
unfamiliar, new to us, traditions:

caramelized creamed onions,
pecan not pumpkin pie,
and dressing with sausage.

Toasting to absent friends with
the best wine of the year,
joining hands for the blessing,

we are a family of friends
together by chance
carving life and turkey.

Next year I'll make Grandma's
lemon meringue pie.

# Pow Wow

Rawhide dresses
swaying gracefully
to fluid movement,
beat of the drums,
husky voices singing
of love and loss,
of rain and sun.

Nothing like this in Wales,
except perhaps the singing.
Denmark's story is rife
with rituals far less civilized
at least so we're told.
Rob Roy and his men
painted their faces, too.

Smoke from the fire
of fresh white sage
rises, cleanses us all.
Hopi, Ute, Navajo,
Welsh, Danish, Scottish,
and makes us Immigrants
long to join the dance circle.

# Smudge

When I moved to Washington,
the District not the State,
a good friend arrived
unannounced from the West
with white sage bundles.
She lit them and smudged each
corner of every room,
"Now it will take care of you,"
she said.

It did.
It became a place of refuge
in a brutal city.  A place for healing.
A place for chocolate chip cookies,
experimental cooking and
*Star Trek: The Next Generation.*
A place for friends to come.
A place for dogs.

When the house was sold
I told the buyer
"This is a good house,
it will take care of you
If you take care of it."
"Is it a family home?"
"No, just a good house,"
I said.

Years later
I drove by to find that he had
knocked out the back walls,
destroyed the deck, the herbs,
the hydrangeas, the perennial
garden, but doubled the
size of the house.

I hope he had someone
smudge it.
That's unlikely.
Perhaps he called in a
pastor, priest, rabbi
or Mormon missionary.

**Well-Traveled Time**

When it strikes the hour, it sounds like someone
hitting a pie tin with a wooden spoon, Great
Grandfather's mantle clock with gilt on the pillars.
> *Tick, tick, tick, tick, tock.*
> *Tick tock, tick tock, tick.*

Made in Connecticut, purchased in Copenhagen,
carried with their few possessions in the stinking
hold of a tossing ship that flew the Danabrog.
> *Tick, tick, tick, tick, tock.*
> *Tick tock, tick tock, tick.*

It was held close and wound, tick tocking their
misery to safe harbor. From steamship to steam
engine, crossing the Missouri to Scotts Bluff.
> *Tick, tick, tick, tick, tock.*
> *Tick tock, tick tock, tick.*

Then west by hand cart, they went a thousand miles
pushing and pulling all they had. The clock ticking,
wrapped in a blanket to keep it safe and keep the time.
> *Tick, tick, tick, tick, tock.*
> *Tick tock, tick tock, tick.*

At the farm house it sat on the mantle, one side too close
to the chimney. The scar is still there. Daughters took it,
handed the clock around teaching children to tell time.
> *Tick, tick, tick, tick, tock.*
> *Tick tock, tick tock, tick.*

It tick-tocked a depression away in Berkeley by the Bay.
A great-grandson brought it back to the mountains
on a slow plane for hours resting in his lap,

once again to teach children. Not so long ago it was
cradled on the back seat of a convertible tick-tocking
across the country once more.
> *Tick, tick, tick, tick, tock.*
> *Tick tock, tick tock, tick.*

Now on the Atlantic coast it counts hours for great-
great-granddaughters who keep it safe, wind it
and listen for it in the night.
> *Tick, tick, tick, tick, tock.*
> *Tick tock, tick tock, tick.*
> *Tong, tong, tong, tong, tong.*

## Grandmother's Coffee Table

Long ago out there in the bright sun
of the rural town the gloom is palpable.
You, as you always did, seek to keep the
furniture untouched. Here in the heart
of the Confederacy, I am overcome
by humidity and wonder how it must
have been for you in that dry, dry place.
Grandmother, what was it like in that
tiny town filled with Mormon men
and their women? In that time,
in that desert, where corn and wheat
must be irrigated and people must not.

I am strong because you were strong.
But why did you convince my Mother,
your daughter, that good things were
not for her and were only for you?
Everything you had was the best
even when it wasn't. It was the best
because it was yours. You were
convinced of that, and told all of us.
You became your possessions.

Today, in my living room
I have the Stickley coffee table
You told my first grade self that
I had destroyed – DESTROYED –
with my jacks. Even then I knew
that destroyed means blown up.
The table was right there.
It still is. Complete with scratches.
The single cherry wood plank
is still two and a half inches thick.

*It is not destroyed. It is an antique,*
*distressed by a little girl's jacks.*

# Aunt Helen's 1966 Mustang

There was nothing special
about it when she drove
it off the lot with 4 miles
on the odometer.
It did have
under-dash air conditioning,
rare then even in Arizona.
And an aquamarine interior,
a new color that year.
Although it had AC, she
drove it very little in the heat
of the Phoenix summers.
When they moved to Salt Lake
she drove it very little in the snow
of the Utah winters.
It was always kept in the garage.

But drive it she did,
to church,
to charity work,
to ceramics classes,
to women's groups,
to pick us up at the airport.
Don't think for one minute that
she didn't use all 271 horses!
I-15 was an experience!
Drive it she did until she was
almost ninety and had
a hip replaced.

Now, because everybody
has a Mustang story,
we take it to car shows.
71,000 miles on the odometer.
It has no after-market parts,
they're all original.
With white exterior well waxed
and gleaming,
and the aquamarine she
chose only slightly worn,

now it's special. A treasure in fact
because it is what it was:
Pure. American.
Aunt Helen's 1966 Mustang.

*Pure. American.*                                                    AMBoyden

WEBoyden, Sr.

## Rx

After Father retired from the big drug company he still
practiced, handsome in the white jacket with his name
        embroidered above the pocket.

He could mix mysterious potions, compounds, elixirs
and emulsions. That's why at home, he was the very best
        gravy-maker ever.

His dispensing beneficent and curative medicines with a joke,
a smile, and a "This will fix you up" made people feel better
        especially when he counted out each capsule,

put them in the bottle, and made a label with his signature,
"Compounded by WB." Father looked after his customers;
        he called them patients.

His store was open 24 hours a day, seven days a week.
"Never live anywhere without a 24-hour pharmacy,"
        he told us.

Often he would call patients with a joke but mostly
just to check on them. Pharmacists don't do that anymore,
        but to Father getting medicine

to people who needed it was not just a business;
        it was a Profession.

## Left Hand Turns

Although she was a Democrat,
Mother avoided left-hand turns.
She would steer clear of them,
driving for blocks, even miles
in what seemed like circular squares.

*"Ma, you passed the street."*
Right turn, right turn, right turn
and there we were.  She had
avoided the danger zipping toward
us on the other side of the road.

We arrived just where
we wanted to be.
Because she was, who she was,
she was seldom afraid,
or so it seemed to us.

She would take on causes,
difficult people, awkward situations
but not oncoming traffic.
With several circumnavigations
before finding parking,

her plan did not consider time.
Seldom punctual, she made
it work for her in more than one city.
In DC, it's impossible, but she
never drove in Washington.

In 15 years of DC driving,
I thought of Mother and
"no left turns" frequently.
This morning running errands,
I found myself plotting

ways to avoid left turns as learned
in AARP Defensive Driving School.
Suddenly, I looked down and saw
Mother's hands on the wheel!
What's up with that!?

## Planting Pansies

Planting pansies
in rich top soil to last the winter,
you are reminded that the best
part of church is singing.

"Come, come, ye Saints,
no toil or labor fear,
but with joy wend your way."

"Little purple pansies,
Touched with yellow gold
Growing in the corner of the garden old,
You are very tiny, but must try, try, try,
Just once more to gladden you and I."

"NO," Mother said.  "It's wrong. When
you sing it, say 'you and me.' It doesn't
rhyme, but it's correct."

Two important lessons:
try without fear and get it right.

## Sunbeams

We owned one of the first Sunbeams.
It was an electric frying pan.
We had it so long that the knob
on the lid cracked and broke off.
We replaced it with the hook from a wire hanger,
needed a hot pad for that one.

Where have all the Sunbeams gone?
There used to be mix masters
in many colors - ours was red.
There were toasters, irons, and
hair dryers with dual blower speeds.

Where have all the Sunbeams gone?
Did they follow the flowers to war?
Does Jesus really want them?
Are they just bankrupt,
or maybe Black and Decker?

# Oxymoronic County

### I
the world is weeping
for abundant poverty
a lot of nothing.

### II
There once was an unfortunate man,
whose vehicle was a Dodge Ram.
Built big and strong,
but something was wrong,
for it leaked lemon juice when it ran.

### III
In a world of contradictions,
it is assumed that any new
creative work is original,
but someone is announcing
"A new classic."
Untested.
Ready to be taped live.
A live performance recorded
and played back unedited.
That's the theory.
My boss says "I will speak my piece
and be forgotten. I will not have
Forgotten to speak my piece."
He thinks it's wise.
Then at the doctor's office
the waiting room is crowded
and the window is closed.
The sign says:
"Please check in at the check-out window."
Sit down dismayed because all of this
Is beginning to make sense.
Sit and wait for the germs to settle on a
contrary world where an ancient magazine
has a story in which
the writer describes a sign announcing
"...an artist's presentation,
'Finding Mystery in Clarity, was this not the
opposite of what most people want..."
Winston Churchill said
"The farther back you can look, the
farther forward you can see."

# Pelican

Fossil records in dusty basements prove
your kind has been around for thirty million years,
for more than a thousand a symbol of faith.

Now when your scoop is on the move,
they realize you're no longer there to tend
the young, allowing the chicks to drink
your blood when rations are scarce.

You are lying in the clean sand of a barrier island,
bill tucked demurely down as in stained glass
at Corpus Christi College or
a Church of St. Thomas Aquinas.

The pelican in her piety.
Wings spread as if in flight, flightless,
sightless. Insects feeding instead of chicks.
The pelican in her passion.

Body of Christ. Wings spread, echoing
crucifixion on the beach at Cape Fear.
A congregation of plovers flies up in salutation.
A descent of woodpeckers strikes the drum.

A fling of sandpipers marches in time.
An overwintering of songbirds sounds the chorus.
An ibis genuflects.

# The "Lady"

She's just too cool and calculating,
too polite to be sincere. Many men
are on a first name basis with her,
and she goes by many names.

She reads signs and portents
the rest of us don't even see.
She calls familiar places
by strange, exotic names.

She tells us to go to the highlighted
route, as if it were an invitation.
Chippenham Parkway becomes
Chip-king-ka-ham and she believes

EAST Duke of Gloucester Street
actually exists. She took us through
the wilds of West Virginia at 35 mph,
adding hours to the trip.

Listen, there are definitely issues. GPS?
More like GPB, now that's rich!
Not to be trusted that
Great Phony *%#&!.

## The Revivalist

On the steps of the Lincoln Memorial a man
      lifts his arms to the heavens. Standing in the place
      where the dream was shared, he shouts that he
      has a nightmare. Thousands cheer.

*"It seems as darkness begins to grow again,*
      *faith is in short supply,"* he rants. Really?
      When did that happen? It seems that people talk
      about God all the time these days.

The whole thing is unreal, surreal, and reel-to-reel.
      Are we asleep? Is this another dream or just satire?
      With a crowd on the Mall, and no one wading in the
      reflecting pool, this day would be parody

if it weren't so filled with hate. It would be satire
      except for the half-cocked conspiracy theories,
      paranoia and lies masquerading as facts.
      Sincerity has been replaced with grandiosity,

eloquence by bravado. He has a right to speak this way,
      but he does not have the right to claim succession
      to Dr. King's inspired vision of a positive future.
      Quite the contrary!

*"Let us not wallow in the valley of despair, I say to you today,*
      *my friends. And so even though we face the difficulties*
      *of today and tomorrow, I still have a dream, It is a dream*
      *deeply rooted in the American dream."*

      Amen.

## Organized Religion

The gray man in a peculiar hat
spoke to me. Familiar, frightening.
I understood the voiceless French
long ago in another country.

The drab man in a cheap blue suit
Spoke down to me. Cloying, condescending.
I did not understand
longer ago in another state.

The polyester woman in pink
Spoke from the porch. Saccharine, superficial.
I understood but could not listen
last year in another town.

The bureaucrat in a three-piece suit
Spoke through the fog. Accented, annoying,
I understand. I am apprehensive
then and there and now and here.

## Crossing Memorial Bridge

It's the long way to the District -- Lee Highway,
Spout Run — rag top folded in the summer
haze -- forested gully, mist clings to trees,
there are surely ghosts here.
Parkway, Roosevelt Island, Arlington
roundabout. In heavy summer haze
the eternal flame flickers above
Lincoln's Doric temple. In every season,
this drive is a pilgrimage. A pilgrimage
to November 25, 1963 -- limbers and caisson,
flag draped casket, color guard, riderless horse.
Gilded stallions bear witness to grief.
Black limousines fill the bridge —
mourners, schemers, dictators, presidents,
politicians, a widow and two brothers.
The world is changed forever.
Still, every morning, after all these years,
the flame burns on the hill.

AMBoyden

## FDA says OK

The FDA says it's OK
to eat the flesh of
cloned animals.
The FDA says cloned
flesh is no different
from the meat people eat
every day in America.
So, apparently,
cloned standing rib
roast clogs arteries.
Cloned country ham
elevates blood pressure.
And fat from cloned
lamb chops coats lips,
the roofs of mouths.
Who knows what else
gets all gummed up.
The FDA says it's OK
to be a vegetarian.

## Food Personified

Chocolate candy talks,
yellow has peanuts, red does not.
The brown one is a girl.
Fulsome chickens sing and dance
trying out for the Chicken Club.
Charlie the Tuna never did
get caught and processed.
Holsteins paint billboards
and wear sandwich boards:

"eat mor chikin"

Shredded wheat goes to school
keeping kids alert and focused.
Carrots, cucumbers, and tomatoes
march into the bowl. Dressing pours
down, they all get tossed.
A disembodied voice urges
"Run Meat Run."
Even water is talking
about being PUR.

There's nothing left to eat.

## transit authority

sun fish sail
away grand cypress
floating softly
in blue with green
not far for white
and dimpled balls
for sticks of graphite
and titanium for the
multicolored striped
full-breasted beginning
of a god-damed stupid
television commercial
mind blank pocket empty
save the quacks for
others who don't know
don't care don't feel
don't want to ride the bus
with two seas like a kiss
which really is better
than a bus unless you are
into buslove
not sunfishlove.

## NOT FORGOTTEN

Dream of things you should have left behind.
Things so far in the past that they are archeology.

Dream of places you should have never gone.
Places where you've never been and yet know.

Dream of people you should have forgotten.
Get up in the night to wind the clocks.

AMBoyden

Bosu balanced, knees bent,
see your toes, weight left,
weight right; suddenly
the air is cold and your legs
remember Regulator Johnson.

The clammy physical therapy
gym dissolves, leaving mountains
beneath and all around,
breathtakingly steep and white,
lift chairs swaying above.

Driving through summer on a steep
deciduous pass; come a tight curve;
hemlock fades as your soul remembers
fragrant spruce, balsamroot and
fireweed in Albian Basin.

Staring out over the Atlantic, gulls
calling, the wide sky impossibly blue
but you need to see Olympus, Sundial,
Timpanogos rising from the horizon
to keep you safe, to bring you home.

## Swamp Cooler

The swamp cooler hums, sucking desert
air through wet straw down into the room.
The dormer is open. A bird calls; traffic begins;
leaves of summer are still, no breeze,
only the promise of heat.

Over the bed that belonged to grandfather,
the high, sloped ceiling follows the double
slant of the roof. Dark beams of solid oak,
stark against white stucco, reflect solstice
sun on the morning of the longest day.

Today is the first dawn with no one
here but me, except of course
the sleeping poodle, her black curly side
slowly rising and falling as the moist air
blows down on us from the vent.

## Oly

Goodbye old friend,
we've gone a long
way together, crossed
bridges over the Potomac,
literal and symbolic;
assaulted the sheer incline
of the Cumberland Gap.
You stayed in your basement digs
When I went away for weekends,
sometimes longer, and always
welcomed me back.
The times you were sick,
we found the best care
not thinking about the expense.
At the Olympics we escaped the bomber;
at Dollywood a woman with big hair
tried to steal you away. In Canada
we were confused by the metric system
and you got locked out in the rain.
The time has come to think
about the expense, but
big, strong, comfortable,
you will serve your new friends
well, even after almost
one hundred and seventy thousand miles.
I will remember you, Oly Volvo.

## Swing Thoughts

The best swing thought
is no swing thought.
Low and slow and
follow through.

Look at the back of the ball,
open your stance.
play the ball back,
use your shoulders.

Don't look up!
Carry the water --
Lateral hazard --
Nuts!

Two club lengths
no nearer the hole.
Feel your left elbow.
Flop it up there

know it's going in,
make it a draw.
Oh shit!
Two inches behind the ball

short back swing.
Look at the target
look at the ball
and swing.

Straight down hill
right at the flag,
hear the ball drop.
High five!

## OLYMPIC TRIALS

With solid breath
In the start house
Stomp bindings
Grab poles
GO GO GO GO GO
Shouted or imagined?
Olympic trials on
New powder
                    Over ice.
Alta
Wildcat      v
                e
                    r
                        t
                            i
                                c
                                    a
                                        l
                                        DROP.
Knees bent.
                    Weight back
*Snow and sky fly by.*
Left gate
                    Right gate
Left gate
                    Right gate
Carved turns
                e
            n
        r
    o
    b
    r
    i
A                   LAND HARD

63

Left gate
                    Right gate
Left gate
                    Right gate
Catch an edge
            Falling
                    Summersaults
                            Bindings don't release.
**SLAM INTO A TREE!**
                    **CRACK**
            Can not move.
            Don't feel cold.
            Ski Patrol.
            Strikker frame.
            Wheelchair.

*white boats float*                                                     AMBoyden

indolent creek moves
into green blue yellow marsh
    tethered white boats float


blue butterfly still
on a blue butterfly bush
    waits for warming sun


blue heron fishes
tranquil wet lands' deep shadows
    in late afternoon


flows the wide river
around towering ferry
    with following gulls

**AMBoyden**

Bluenose in the sun
  heeled over lee rail under
    racing with gulls

  running down wind
    loaded with scallops and cod
      no mere racing ship

    from forest primeval
      two raked masts
        all sails drawing

      Nova Scotia's own
        last of the Grand Banks schooners
          alive on a dime

copper sun
        setting in the sea
night heron calls

        moon washed beach
drift wood could
        be bones of poets

maritime forest
        bent by wind and spray
red fox runs

        corn snake slithers
live oak lives
        past is present

**Bald Head Island**

*Maritime Forest*                                                    AMBoyden

## Masks

There are places where
masks, mysteries and riddles
make fools of angels.

Places where a mask
covers secret with secret
wrapped in mystery.

Places where riddles
may reveal enigmas
but cannot be solved.

Places where her mask,
created by Mary Kaye,
envelops her soul

Places where his mask,
chiseled by testosterone,
hides his compassion.

Places filled with masks
by Italian designers --
modern rituals.

Ambition demands
a mask for each occasion.
Pretense is success.

## Old Riddle

If you have it,
You don't share it.
If you share it,
You don't have it.
The question is
Who wants it?
And why?

## Camouflage

The mask he has worn for sixty years
has begun to chafe the sides of his jaw.
Although it is able to grow its own beard,
smile broadly and twinkle its eyes --
he longs to rip it off, toss it aside
revealing loneliness and fear,
desperation and depression.
Instead he presses the mask in place
as he turns to greet another one
who wants something from him,
who knows something about him,
who takes away the best of him.
The mask has protected him
like a fencer's from drawn rapier,
like a bee keeper's from stings,
like a soldier's camouflage.
Protected him from hurled harm
like a catcher's or a goalie's.

Now it chafes.
He yanks at it.
It won't come.

## E.D.

Drug sellers have no compunction
with ads for erectile dysfunction
because blue Viagra
is a cash flow Niagara.
Please someone! Get an injunction!


## Lily's Dilemma

There once was a poodle named Lily,
Who thought that her boyfriend was silly,
A shih tzu named Guinness
Was "fixed" in his "biness"
Miss Lily thought *Won't he or will he?*


## The Big Myth

Pocahontas and Captain John Smith
Never had a romance! It's a myth!
When she's just eleven
He's at least twenty-seven
Tell Cole Porter and Disney, forthwith.


## Election Year

Davenport, Danville, to Dover
candidates promise us clover.
We're in the same boat!
It's true, we must vote,
but wake me when it's all over


## OOOPPPS!

His wife's birthday, Jonathan Dirk,
purchased a card, left it at work.
A card, not a gift?!
No wonder she's miffed
She's sorry she married a jerk!

## Who Knows?

Do you think they know
they aren't outside,
those birds who live in Lowes?

Do you think they know
their pals have died
those mutts and calicos?

Do you think they know
they're on a ride,
those folks who wait in rows?

Do you think they know
who's on their side,
those men who come to blows?

Do you think they know
each pallid bride
there are no bright rainbows?

# Guilt is for the Birds

A long time ago, in the first grade
I had a canary who did not sing.
Father said it was because the
bird was a girl. But I thought
she just didn't want to.
I loved her as first graders will.
But one week forgot to
give her food and water
as first graders will.
She died.
I felt terrible. Still do.

Later I had a canary named
Bubbles Silverman
Who sang with *Hee Haw* and
the Mormon Tabernacle Choir.
I took very good care of him,
gave him special food
and a tonic for his throat.
One day while singing
Bubbles keeled over
reaching a high note.
He died.
I felt terrible.  Still do.

Much later I had four
brightly colored little finches,
named Huey, Dewey, Louie
and d'Artagnan, who lived
in a bamboo cage in my kitchen.
I even took them to the vet.
One day they got out of the cage,
slipped right through the bars.
Four little birds are simply
no match for two big dogs.
They died.
I felt terrible. Still do.

Much, much later
I had a grey cheek parrot,
named Senator Robert Bird,
who sat on my head
when I wrote. He thought
he was a dog and
learned their language,
conversing with them at length.
He was funny and friendly and
I had him for twenty-five years.
The vet said that was remarkable
for a grey cheek parrot.
One morning he fell
off his perch.
He died.
I felt terrible. Still do.

In the last third of my life
I have come to know
that grief is unavoidable,
a part of being alive.
I have also learned that
unlike compassion or regret,
guilt is manufactured.
Still, no more caged birds.
I'll feed and enjoy the
wild ones in the yard.

## Knowing

I don't know
what all these others
seem to know for sure.
What all these others keep
shouting at all the rest of us.

I do know all the words to all
the songs played at piano bars
but can't sing anymore.

I know that when the hurricane
comes again, and the lights go out
I will be afraid.

I know that helpless and in pain
again, in an emergency room,
I will be terrified.

I know that when for the first time,
I swing from the tee and the ball
goes in the hole,
I will be ecstatic.

## Last Afternoon

After breaking ninety on Blue Heron, I will tell you
I love you and walk the dog on her aromatic route.

Someone will answer all fifteen questions correctly
and take home the million dollars. It might be me.

We will open a bottle of Opus One to celebrate.
Cut a wheel of aged cheddar and one of brie.

There will be artichokes and silver queen corn,
love, chocolate, and very thin sugar cookies.

We'll play the original cast album of *South Pacific,*
the one with Mary Martin and Ezio Pinza.

The standard poodle will have liver and chicken
and I will prepare it on the last afternoon of my life.

But you see, I won't know it's the last.

## They Stop the Heart

"They stop the heart, you know,"
she said as if it were an
every day occurrence.

But then they start it again.
apparently with those paddles,
just as they do on television.

"It's supposed to return the
heart to normal rhythm,"
she says dispassionately.

It's like rebooting a computer
except that people do say,
"My hard drive is dead."

Why is it that people speak of
fearsome conditions and their cures
without personal pronouns?

"The liver is involved."
"They stop the heart."
"The lung will be removed."

Not his liver nor my liver.
Not her heart nor my heart.
Not his lung nor my lung.

With no she or my,
no he or I, no one
possesses the thing.

If it's just some organ
floating around out there
disembodied, is it less frightening

not to own the affliction?
How could someone ever say:
"They are going to stop my heart."

## THAT IS REAL
### *March 1989*

Insurance card in fist
I come. Pain in chest.
"Take her back now," they say.
But my heart isn't broken.
It's something else,
and they send me home,
where it gets worse.
Breathing becomes precious.
So I return to the unknown hospital.
It's the infection they say
that killed the Muppet man.

Three weeks unaware.
Not really.
I feel the ventilator,
see the faces,
hear the singing.
Is it real, the singing?
There's a bass,
a baritone,
a soprano,
but the song doesn't go anywhere.
Is it because
I don't know where I am?

And the faces, are they real?
Kathleen, Walt, Bill, Ned, Dan, Bob?
Shauna, Julie, Jed, Ted, Dot, Steve?
Some are more here than others.
Some are real. But which?
This is truly alone.
I've been alone before,
but this is far point now,
surrounded by people alone.
Uncovered, voiceless.

They talk about me
in the third person,
I shout, "I'm in here,"
but the tube.
Doctors come and go.
"Good Morning,
I'm the lung doctor."
*Damn, I know that!*

There's a clock and a calendar.
A television and the sea sounds,
a voice tells me that it's
an exclusive club,
those who hear the sea sounds.

These sea sounds are not real.
This singing is not real.
Some faces are not real.
My pain is real.
The drugs are real.
My fear is real.
Hope is real.

# Requiem in Common Time

### One
The time you said to me
"I'm proud of you,
the way you've lived your life."
I should have said,
"Do you believe in one way to be?"

You taught me algebra;
no one else could.
Is there a formula?
An equation?
An unintelligible peal scheme?

Then nine tailors,
and ninety-seven more.
I should have said,
"Thank you, I love you too."
Maybe I did.

### Two
That time I died
I didn't see the light
or tunnel or winged being.
Gloria in excelsis.

A child of sound,
that time I died,
I heard The Mormon Tabernacle Choir,
a great featherbed of sound

multi-layered, big and soft.
Crescendo. Diminuendo.
Spongy and sheltered, in eight parts.
whooosh, plunk. hisssss, clunk -

or was it the ventilator?
That time I died
I didn't count three hundred voices.
There was one. Full forte.

Incapable of pianissimo.
I can never understand the words.
No one can.
D.C. *Al fine.*

That time I died, I didn't.

### Three
Today they laid the grass down
smooth and dry on eighteen feet
of the valley floor by box elders
and Lucy's having been there.

Now the son of a treble shawm
lies silent. Sweet sound gone
wherever charmers go.
Serene Oboe d'amore.

Tomorrow they will lay
a Beta gentleman worthy of the name
in another place where an oboe
mourns.

### Four
Emily says
it's a gentleman,
who kindly stops.

Wolfgang feared it,
and wrote a score for it.
So did Leonard.

The Harvard Guru says,
"One year is the same thing."
Or is it a woman

carrying spring tulips,
and a beginning?
My very good friend says,

"I respect death.
it's the only thing that could
kill my Mother
and all those
times I wanted to."

**AMBoyden**

it's hard not to think
      when mother was just my age
cardiac arrest.

## Email from a Friend

The subject line is: "I've moved into hospice."
The message explains Lou Gehrig's
disease, breathing and feeding tubes,
"all the bells and whistles."

He has chosen to remove all life sustaining
aids in one week's time. He's been told
his life will then end within 24 hours.

He tells us, "You are among my many dear friends
and I cherish our relationship forever. Farewell!"

This morning another email from his son.
Our friend died this morning, peacefully.
A tragically sad, touching to tears,
graceful goodbye.


*"Because death would not stop for him*
*He kindly stopped for death."*

## Funerals

Too many funerals,
in graceful buildings,
new or historic, formal,
stilted, with a choir, and
eulogies by someone who
didn't know the deceased.

Too many funerals,
celebratory, new age, with
a release of balloons,
a Piute prayer wheel, and a
jazz combo. People one by one
sharing memories of the dead.

Too many funerals,
singing of hymns, reading of
barely relevant scriptures, and
long speeches by leaders who
may have known the departed
and food from church ladies.

Too many funerals.
Today at the dead woman's
home where a priest read a
psalm and the husband greeted
invited guests with
catered food but no music.

Too many funerals,
perfect markers in perfect rows.
Stacked two to a grave, the one who dies
last gets to be on top. Prayers, flags,
guns and an Air Force Band honor
tradition along with the fallen.

Too many funerals,
all for those still breathing.
Out to Coalville they said, "People are
dying who've never died before."

# Chased by a Hurricane

The pool became a pond,
the pond a lake,
the lake an ocean

held back by concrete walls built
by the Army Corps of Engineers.
Hugo and Beatrice, Floyd and Isabel,

Ernesto and Hanna emptied the heavens,
toppled the trees and changed our lives.
Then came Irene. Storms

with names are ruthless. Christened,
they live. Pursue to destroy.
She was twelve hours behind us

in Parsippany. We were unaware,
so stopped to sleep. Irene did not.
Six hours behind in Lenox.

We stopped at Tanglewood to listen.
Irene did not. She chased us to Bennington
and Londondary. Still we didn't know,

so visited a gallery, lingered over lunch.
Irene did not. She almost caught
us in Ludlow. She flooded the town,

doused the lights, destroyed bridges,
washed out roads. Up on the mountain
safe in an elegant ski lodge, we slept.

## Orange and Maroon Morning

One cold orange and maroon mountain morning
a man with two guns, some chains and a grudge
comes to change a safe world without warning.
He thinks he's been dissed. He's come here to judge.

He has come to destroy not to create.
He's just not accountable. It's not his fault.
He's come for revenge and won't hesitate.
For everyone else has caused this assault.

Painters use oils. Composers use tone.
Writers use words, but this man uses guns.
This man is a blamer who wants blood and bone.
What he'll do today cannot be undone.

Silent and careful in planning the deed,
for the first time ever, today he'll succeed.

## Unconvinced

You are all so certain.
You write of god as if you know one.
Your words ring with conviction.
I am unconvinced.

Is conviction always courageous?

Was it courageous to fly airplanes
filled with people into buildings
filled with people?
I am unconvinced.

## MOOSE

For a thousand years this has been our home
between jutting peaks on snowbound meadows.
Granite summits rise from the valley floor into
the chill of a winter sky and we have been here.

With foxes, rabbits, squirrels, and ferrets,
pronghorns, coyotes and trumpeter swans.
With snakes, lizards, elk and deer,
black bears who play and bears who walk upright.

With wildcats, bison, eagles and bighorn sheep.
Wolves had been here, now they are back.
For a thousand years we have been here,
with moss on our antlers, watching the cows and calves.

We clear the snow to find frozen winter grass,
seeking shelter in the forest when cold night comes.
The two-legged ones came with their bows.
They wanted to kill us, but we survived.

The two-legged ones came with guns and bullets.
They wanted to kill us, but we survived
Now the two-legged ones come stinking, half machine
making thunder and ugly tracks in the crusted snow.

We may not survive.
Who will be here in a thousand years?

# Spring Doves

Round brown bodies,
bright black eyes,
and white spats
for cocktail hour.

It's just natural
for them to come
each afternoon
five-ish, for drinks.

"I'll meet you there."
They've made a date.
The watering hole
is pretty and posh.

He puffs up and
she pecks his cheek.
Sitting on the railing,
billing and cooing

not caring who sees.
Then in a flutter
as they came,
they go, until tomorrow.

As the courting
Continues,
"Get a nest!"
says the bartender.

So they did.
Not much later
they start bringing
kids for dinner.

Then the kids start
bringing new friends
for cocktail hour.
And so it goes.

## Hummingbird

I held a hummingbird in my hand.
There was nothing there but life.
A perfect creature bound by silk
rescued from a spider's lair.
I pulled the sticky tangles from his
long beak, little feet, tiny silver
tail, and at last his wings.
Suddenly he flew.

Later I saw him at the feeder.
There was a silver thread
hanging from his back.
He hovered in midair
with bright blue wings a blur,
he looked me in the eye,
and flew away.

## OLD POEMS

I am history in a teacup with dregs in the bottom.
Decades pass. I yellow in an ancient brown folder.
Unblinking scenes from times and places best forgotten,
or are they? I wait for light and air and a dry martini.
There are loves and losses followed by a rhyming couplet.

I am a salamander lying where night thoughts hover.
My maker disappeared, vanished, gone undercover.

I am life in a chipped and empty Coca-Cola bottle.
Years go by and I remain in a tattered three-ring binder.
Unadulterated feelings, fragments of old emotions
lie in me waiting for the right moment and a nice red wine.
I am death in the dusty bottom drawer of a roll-top desk.

In the end, when I am discovered, I will have my revenge.

## Déjà New

Experts have found the brain
circuit that may cause déjà vu.
Now you can understand why
you think it's happened before,

but don't know where or when.
Scientists report that the eerie
experience of knowing you have
had this conversation,

been in this room,
heard this music,
kissed this man before,
is the result of a conflict

between two parts of your brain.
They say this research
will lead to a cure for experiencing
things already seen, if it needs curing.

Will it also cure tedium,
or being bored on a grey day
when the sky is lifeless?
Of course the drug meant to cure

could have a side effect:
creating the opposite illusion where
the familiar is new and strange.

# Down Under Dreaming

Take the water taxi across the harbor
to the Opera House and *Carmen*
in a ship it took fifteen years
to launch.

Utzen's ship under full sail
on the edge of the harbor.
Sing *Advance Australia Fair*
or *Waltzing Matilda* -- whichever --
at the start of a football game.

Encounter penguins marching
on the sand with surf lapping around
their flat feet.
Visit **Giurgola's** Parliament House
where the giant green and gold flag flies
on four huge legs over Canberra

and **Lake Burley Griffin,**
named for the American who
designed the capital city,
just as a Frenchman designed
Washington. All of them sites
to see.

Dreams ever since graduate school
when a classmate came from Sydney.
He had curly blond hair, a perfect tan,
and said "crikey" before it was a fad.
I haven't made it but still wonder
what it's like to dine by candlelight
in a rain forest.

Is Alice Springs like Ely, Nevada?
Is Perth just like Chicago?
Is Melbourne San Francisco?
And Sydney New York?
I hope not. I've been to all those other places.
Have you ever danced to a didgeridoo?

It isn't perfect -- yet it's perfect --
Tangled snarled ancient beautiful --
August Roses bloom full
Anticipating chubby Daffodils --
Her little Sexton sings again —
Bees find flowers they prefer —
September Daylilies paint
Dashing strokes foretelling
Iris in May  --  on the lawn
Dandelion tales – Brawny Oak
Reaches for the sky as we
Find where it's been —
Ready to burst rusty buds
On giant Magnolias signal rebirth --
In the woods delicate Lady's Slippers
Or papery Trillium greet descendants
Of snakes and Poisonous plants
That led Emily to discover -- not goblins  --
only angels --

AMBoyden

**Homage following a visit to
Emily Dickinson's Garden
where her words still live.**

## Face in the Fog

As the fog begins to clear
a stranger's face stares back
from the deep dark.
Where is this face, lost in an
embarrassment of guilt?
Who is it, this lost face?
Is it someone from yesterday?
Or someone from tomorrow?
All yesterdays were once tomorrows,
and losing face can
happen then or now or next.
Why is it staring
as the fog begins to clear?

# Dropped Names

In my bed and on PBS, I learn that on this day
Phyllis McGinley was born in Oregon.
I thought she was from Utah.
I spoke to her once - on the telephone.

In Starbucks and *The New York Times,* I learn
Barbara Guest is gone. Isn't she dead already?
So long. I never spoke to her,
in person or on the telephone.

In stereo and in my brain, Cleo Lane sings
my way to work. "The Compleat Works of Shakespeare,"
no kidding! Accompanied by her husband,
John Dankworth, and his orchestra.

At work and in my boots I quote Captain John Smith,
who was in the Army and did not marry Pocahontas.
She married John Rolfe. Cole Porter didn't know,
neither did Walt Disney.

In the rough and on eighteen, it's late in the game,
I look at the target; look at the ball; and swing.
Bob Rotella teaches that.
Nancy Lopez says, "Look at the back of the ball."

On the way home I see a sign:
"Whose woods these are?"
Well, naturally I think I know.

## Elegy for a Cardinal

This morning Ricky died.
He owned this house although
he had never been inside.
His bright red personality
banged into windows,
and inspected us while
hanging on the screens.
He dined on seed and suet,
showing beautiful reddish brown
Lucy the way to the food.
A true Virginia gentleman,
he protected his home and family,
including us. He was
in charge when the dog,
Lily, was away.

This morning a hawk
swooped down and grabbed him.
Lily and I witnessed the awful
deed from the kitchen.
He was looking right at me,
asking for help. I couldn't get
there before the hawk flew off.
Maybe the hawk dropped him
when it found he wasn't a mouse.
Lily knew it was not true.

Violence came onto our deck
When Ricky died this morning.
We don't know where the hawk
took him so we can't bury him
underneath the birdbath.
Lucy and the babies mourn,
so do we.

## Lily Goodbye

From the day you arrived you made us laugh,
and you brought with you a new kind of grace.
Tight curls, black eyes, tiny feet, worried face,
you seemed not to mind when having a bath.
Took over our lives, kit and caboodle
sat at the table and slept in our beds,
ruled the roost - not very well bred,
who really cares; no peer has a poodle.

As the years sped by you became slower.
The race up the drive became a mere trot.
Squirrels all got lazy; they thought you were gone.
Bright eyes grew dim and sharp ears dropped lower.
The trot was a mosey; you could not hear a shot,
but still made us laugh, loved us and milk bones.

**With apologies to
Giacomo da Lentini ,
Phyllis McGinley,
and Julia Child**

## What Would Jung Think?

The shrill shriek of wind
signals the beginning of the end.
The dying willow weeps as the pond
fills with empty cans, old tires,
plastic bottles, cast-off furniture.

In the back seat of a speeding 1950
Dodge Wayfarer the lone passenger
suddenly realizes there is no driver.
The car is racing toward the pond
where the willow weeps.

The Dodge is out of control. Frozen,
the passenger watches as the willow
comes closer. Then stiffly, with great
effort, the rider struggles over the bench
seat back and slides down into

the driver's place. Slamming down
on the brake pedal, pulling
the emergency handle up
and up, the passenger/driver stops,
teetering on the edge. Pouring rain

and thunder, lightning strikes the tree
as the unstable car starts sliding down
the bank into the water. The rider
rolls down a window, readies to
squirm out -- and wakes.

yellow swing swings
yellow bird flies
threatening yellow sky


heavy heart sinks
into bitter winter
of the weary soul


moonless middle of the longest night
dogs sleep dreaming
worried humans wake

**AMBoyden**

where is all the snow
to touch souls, spin tires
watch wait

silent snowflakes
covering mistakes with white
ice cracks and groans

still does cross
walking on point
three ballerinas

polaris guides us
captain newport's
star ships

taurus charges
across the night sky
raging for respect

orion rising
ready raging bull
belt with three stars

scorpio rising
orion sets
not sharing sky

## The Trouble with Reading Cookbooks

Open the book with beautiful pictures of wonderful food
and suddenly there you are in a Williams-Sonoma apron
with a fresh fruit and whole fish pictorial. It's pockets big
enough for a wooden spoon, if you ever put one there.

Line up prep bowls, whisk at the ready, food processor
out and ready to whirr. All set for *Chilled Avocado Soup
with Seared Chipotle Shrimp.* Nobody likes chipotle.
Someone is allergic to shrimp. So maybe *Linguine*

*with Two Cheese Sauce.* Heck, that's just mac 'n' cheese,
but harder to eat with the long pasta. Here's a good one:
*Salmon Cakes with Sorrel Sauce.* It uses canned salmon,
that's in the pantry, but where do you get sorrel?

Certainly not on the deck with the other herbs. OK,
here's the one: *Beet Wellington!* There's phyllo dough
in the freezer, beets in the crisper, rosemary and thyme
in a pot. Roast the beets; find mushrooms in the fridge.

Run across the street for an egg, sauté the mushrooms,
add dried shallots, you don't have fresh; slice the beets;
run next door for walnuts; arrange all the good stuff
on the dough. Roll them and glaze with the whipped egg.

Put the pretty little packages in a 375° oven for 25 minutes,
until golden brown. Set the table, steam asparagus, warm rolls,
toss salad, put away the food processer you didn't use,
and call everyone to dinner.

Someone says "Please pass the salt."
You should have made your own mac 'n' cheese.

## Fortune Cookie

The fortune says:
"Anger begins with folly, and ends with regret."

What does this mean?
"Anger begins with folly…"
Foolishness, idiocy, stupidity,
just plain dumbness
can all make a person angry.
mad even.

"…and ends with regret."
Well now! That's really stupid!
Never be sorry for being angry,
only for showing it
or for acting on it

Like the legendary time
when I threw everything
on my desk across the room.
My assistant came in
with a wry smile and said,
"Did you want these things filed?"
I laughed.

## Turning Name

Lazy ceiling fans turning above
people laboring over steaks
and pasta in an antique hardware
store refitted as a restaurant
without air conditioning.

Turning, turning, turning.
Psychotic people hear
voices calling their names
as I do here in the heat
of a June evening while

the caesar salad wilts,
the fans turn too slowly.
Different timbre, different tone
soprano alto tenor bass.
A quartet is calling me

over calamari, clam sauce
and clatter of chatter and dishes.
Turning, I see a table of four,
two men, two women
all mouthing my name

over and over and over.
They don't like the person
whose name they repeat
again and again and again
in a baroque counterpoint.

Turning back to the wilting salad
under the lazy ceiling fans
I wonder if it's true that all
any of us has is our good name.

What right do these
distasteful overdone others
have to my name, anyway?

"Are you speaking of me?"
I ask.

### At Eb & Flo's Steam Bar

Two tall women sitting on
two tall chairs at a tall
table telling too tall tales
to each other
over steamed clams
and french fries.
One with hair like a
black watch cap and
a black turtle neck.
The other with long
blond curls and
a soft blue sweater.
They never stop talking.
What rumors are they spreading?
What gossip do they share?
What secrets come and go
here at Eb & Flo's?

## Nether Niners

They sit around the table,
the nether niners,
carping and moaning.

The little one.
The chic one.
The short one.

They speak in absolutes.
"The hats are stupid."
"The potatoes are cold."

Their opinions are clear.
"Nothing is good."
"Nothing is right."

There they sit.
Are they happy
clucking and cooing?

The dull one.
The sly one.
The nasty one.

Deliciously gossiping:
"She is leaving for a pro."
"He's broke after the fall."

Piously fawning:
"Poor man, he is dying."
"Poor dear, he's her burden."

Maliciously taunting:
"You should be embarrassed."
"You have nothing but time."

Here I am in mismatched sox.
It's perfect, perfectly unpleasant.
It is not a game.

# Faux Toile

The woman strides purposely toward
a corner table; her faux toile dress in
black and white clings tightly
to her muffin top and sagging breasts.
Spaghetti straps press into her soft shoulders.
It's "All You Can Eat Crab Legs Night."

A younger woman with a sweater draped
over her shoulders because of the air
conditioning sucks on a leg as the pile
of crustation carcasses in the middle
of the table grows. Outside the temperature
is ninety-nine degrees.

Are the two friends, sisters, lovers?
Or is the younger one the faux-toile
woman's daughter? Hair the same bleached
blond, noses alike, they stand up to leave.
The younger one pulls off her sweater
and throws it over her arm.

She wears a too tight tank top that reveals nipples
and navel. Her skirt is appropriate to a production
of *Swan Lake*. Seriously, it's a tutu!
Now it's clear: mother and daughter,
with the same nose and the same
taste in fashion.

## "You're Welcome"

"No problem."
"It's nothing."
"My pleasure."
"You bet."

**Translations:**

"No problem" -
Generally you are a pain
but this time not so much.

"It's nothing" -
This may be important to you,
but it means diddly to me.

"My Pleasure" -
My boss told me to say that,
but if you think bringing you
a grilled cheese sandwich
is a pleasure, you have
another think coming.

"You bet"
Huh?

These responses are disingenuous
at best, contemptuous at worst

Instead of "Thank you" –

"Maybe next time."
"No problem."

"Nice try."
"It's nothing."

"This is burned!"
"My pleasure."

"Never mind."
"You bet."

"You're welcome" may be
insincere, but at least it's
learned in kindergarten,
or not.

## Valentine

Her bright blue phone vibrates.
The girl with the auburn hair
listening to the man droning on
about the War of 1812 slips
the phone from her pocket
and glances down at the screen
without tipping her head.

"b my v tine
c u   luv J"

The girl with the auburn hair
and the fancy phone
feels her heart beating and smiles.
There is no lace doily or
hearts or red roses,
no chocolate or diamonds.
but as far as the girl
with the auburn hair is concerned
J cared enough to send the very best.

WEBoyden, Sr.

## My Pup and I

I take my puppy for a ride
  He always likes to go.
I pet his head and scratch his back
  Because he likes it so.

Our race track reaches round the block
  It seems it never ends
And we can ride and ride and ride
  And talk to all our friends.

We have some secrets of our own
  And we can laugh and shout
And talk of all the things we find
  While riding all about.

# Acknowledgments

## Images

All images except the following were made by Ann Marie Boyden.
All photographs on Page 16 were taken at the Museum of Modern Art, New York

vii. AnnEtta and Ann Marie back at the Pi Phi House
An unknown collegiate member of Utah Alpha,
Pi Beta Phi

6. *Dodging and Burning*
Coalville, Utah circa 1900
Walter Mitchell Boyden
Print by Ann Marie Boyden

14. *Mother Used to Write Poetry*
Frances Marie Nuttall - Wedding Portrait
Lignell and Gill, 1935, Salt Lake City

17. *The Starry Night*, St. Rémy, June, 1898
Vincent van Gogh (1853-1890)
Oil on Canvas, 29" x 36 1/4" (73.7 x 92.1 cm)
Acquired through the Lillie P. Bliss Bequest
Museum of Modern Art , NY, U.S.A.
Digital Image © The Museum of Modern Art
Licensed by SCALA/Art Resource, NY

18. *Dieppe, Bassin Duquesne, low tide, morning sun*
Camille Pissarro
Oil on canvas 54.5 x 65 cm, R.F. 1937-55
Musée d'Orsay, Paris, France
Photo Credit: Erich Lessing/Art Resource, NY

19. *The First Impressionist*
*The Red Roofs or Corner of a Village, Winter* – 1877
Also known as *Los Techos Rojos Del Pueblo en Inviero*
Camille Pissarro
Oil on canvas 54.5 x 65.5 cm
Musée d'Orsay, Paris, France
Photo Credit: Erich Lessing/Art Resource, NY

23. *Manga*
Japanese Calligraphy, 1789

45. *Rx*
Medical Arts Pharmacy Window
Circa 1938
Walter Everett Boyden, Sr.

112. *My Pup and I*
Walter Everett Boyden, Sr.
Printed in the Deseret News
Salt Lake City, 17 May 1943

115. *Cape Fear, North Carolina*
Kathleen C. Egelund

# Quotations

9. *Its Magic*
Jule Styne and Sammy Cahn
*from Romance on the High Seas*
Marvin Gaye
*Let's Get It On*

12. *Prologue to the Canterbury Tales*
Geoffrey Chaucer

47. *Planting Pansies*
*Come, Come Ye Saints*
Text: William Clayton (1814-1879)
Music: English Folk Song
*Hymns of the The Church of Jesus
Christ of Latter Day Saints*
*Little Purple Pansies*
Text: Anonymous.
Music: Joseph Ballantyne
(1868-1944)
*Children's Songbook, The Church of
Jesus Christ of Latter Day Saints*

49. "...an artist's presentation,
'Finding Mystery in Clarity,' was this
not the opposite of what most
people want..."
Amy Hemple
*What Were the White Things?*

52. *The Revivalist*
Reverend Martin Luther King, Jr.
From *I Have a Dream* Speech

59. "mountains are calling..."
Chris Highland, John Muir
*The Meditations of John Muir:
Nature's Temple*

85. *email from a friend*
Robert J. Cowling, AIA
email from an architect, poet, and
musician
Emily Dickinson, J712
Paraphrase of "Because I could not
stop for death..."

96. Emily Dickenson
"...chubby daffodils..." J142
"...little Sexton..." J124
Thomas H. Johnson
*The Complete Poems of Emily
Dickinson*

"...snakes...goblins...angels..."
Dickenson quote
Alfred Habegger
*My Wars Are Laid Away in Books,*
p. 159

100. *Lily Goodbye*
"...kit and caboodle no peer has a
poodle..."
Phyllis McGinley
*Times Three*

112: *My Pup and I*
Almost certainly Frances Nuttall
Boyden
Printed in the *Deseret News*
Salt Lake City, 17 May 1943

*Cape Fear, North Carolina*                              KCEgelund

There are almost four decades of jotting included in this collection. Plus one really old poem that Ann Marie probably didn't write. Some are published. Some won awards. Some are good, all are honest. Many are short, mostly because she spent a career writing commercials and ads. What can be said in ten seconds? Lots, it turns out. Some of the poems will speak to you, make you remember, or make you laugh.

Ann Marie is grateful for the opportunity to live in Williamsburg surrounded by history. She misses the mountains but has come to love the sea.


Williamsburg, Virginia
May 2013